P9-BZE-128

Published by Leah Jay, dba Leah Jay Artworks
Printed in China by Global PSD
First Edition: June 2015

Library of Congress Control Number: 2015907387

ISBN: 978-0-692-44510-5

Visit Leah Jay online at leahjayart.com

AMPHIBIAN LOVE

an artbook by Leah Jay

Firstly, thank you for buying this book. Here's how the project came about:

Two years ago I illustrated a toad and a newt, and brought both as part of my portfolio to a Society of Children's Book Writer's and Illustrator's (SCWBI) Conference. The reviewer preferred the style of those two right away. When I got back to the studio I intended to explore that style and subject further, but realized I hadn't done much initial research. When I did, I learned that I'd painted the cane toad - an invasive, poisonous species in Australia - and a fairly common Californian newt called *Taricha granulosa* - the rough-skinned newt. While researching, I accidentally came across some more information about amphibians in general:

> They consist of five types: frogs, toads, salamanders, newts, and caecilians.
>
> Cold-blooded, they live both in water and on land during different stages of development, lay eggs without shells, and have porous, thin skin. Not surprisingly, they're sensitive to environmental changes. In fact, the overall health of amphibian populations in an area can be an early indicator of a biome under stress.
>
> They are going extinct at unprecedented rates all over the world – from habitat destruction, environmental changes, pollution, competition with invasive species, overcollection for food and the pet trade, and chytridiomycosis, a fungal disease epidemic.

These facts resonated with me, especially as I thought about the state of the Earth's ecosystem... As I started to illustrate my next frog, a deep feeling of caring and sympathy for these animals began to set in. I've always been an artist who enjoyed exploring and painting a wide variety of subjects, but knew that if I found a good reason to choose just one thing, I could paint a series.
It became a personal crusade to illustrate these delightful creatures. I began by saving, with permission, online images from noted photographers and scientists to use as reference. But I wanted to go beyond what photography and traditional scientific illustration could do. Using my free-flowing watercolor and colored pencil style, I highlighted the charm of these creatures, and added a touch of poetry to convey an interesting fact about each one.

The book you hold in your hand represents two years of joyful effort. I hope my pictures will lead you to a greater understanding of the many interesting creatures out there in the world, and evoke a compassionate feeling towards those underappreciated animals we rarely see in our daily lives.

THE AMPHIBIANS

1. Ishikawa's Frog, *Odorrana ishikawae*
2. Spadefoot Toad, *Pelobates fuscus*
3. Axolotl, *Ambystoma mexicanum*
4. Rainbow Burrowing Frog, *Scaphiophryne gottlebei*
5. Cave Salamander, *Eurycea lucifuga*
6. Ringed Caecilian, *Siphonops annulatus*
7. Kihansi Spray Toad, *Nectophrynoides asperginis*
8. Green Salamander, *Aneides aeneus*
9. La Parva Spiny-Chested Frog, *Alsodes Tumultuosis*
10. Long-Toed Salamander (juvenile), *Ambystoma macrodactylum*
11. Imbabura Tree Frog, *Hypsiboas picturatus*
12. Lanza's Alpine Salamander, *Salamandra lanzai*
13. Mr. Burns Beaked Toad, *Rhinella sp. nov.*
14. Spotted Salamander, *Ambystoma maculatum*
15. Betic Midwife Toad, *Alytes dickhilleni*
16. Giant Palm Salamander, *Bolitoglossa dolfeini*
17. Lake Titicaca Water Frog, *Telmatobius coleus*
18. Banded Horned Tree Frog, *Hemiphractus fasciatus*
19. Northern Banded Newt, *Ommatotriton ophryticus*
20. Marsupial Horned Frog, *Gastrotheca cornuta*
21. California Red-Legged Frog, *Rana draytonii*
22. Bornean Rainbow Toad, *Ansonia latidisca*
23. Hochstetter's Frog, *Leiopelma hochstetteri*
24. Rough-Skinned Newt, *Taricha granulosa*

1

Ishikawa's Frog, or *Odorrana ishikawae*

(Reference photo by Shawn Miller)
Endangered status: EN Endangered
Location & habitat: the southern Japanese islands of Amamaioshima and Okinawajima

This species has been called "the most beautiful frog in Japan". It's threatened by development around the forest streams it lives in, particularly by road and dam construction.

Painted in
my brights and spots
I blend
in with
moss,
ferns and rocks

2 Spadefoot Toad, or *Pelobates fuscus*

(Reference photo by Benny Trapp)
Endangered status: LC Least Concern (populations decreasing)
Location & habitat: across eastern Europe

The Spadefoot toad lives in deserts, close to underground water sources with loose, sandy soils. It digs itself backward into the ground to find moisture. By doing this, it can wait a few weeks for the next rain to fall.

the SPADEFOOT TOAD
DIGS IN DEEP
to HIDE IN MUD FOR a WINTER SLEEP

3

Axolotl, or *Ambystoma mexicanum*

Endangered status: CR Critically Endangered
Location & habitat: the southeastern edge of Mexico City, Mexico

The Axolotl is well known for remaining in a larval stage, keeping its external feathery gills and staying underwater for life. Its only known home, the Xochimilco Lake complex, has been deeply affected by the growth of Mexico City.

AXOLOTLS Swimming
PRETTY
IN A LAKE UNDER
MÉXICO CITY

4 Rainbow Burrowing Frog, or *Scaphiophryne gottlebei*

Endangered status: EN Endangered
Location & habitat: in and around the Parque Nacional de Isalo, in southeastern Madagascar

Living in rocky crevices, these frogs are able to withstand floods by hanging on to the rocks with their specially-adapted front feet. They breed quickly and take advantage of temporary pools of water that may dry up within weeks to lay eggs. Because these frogs are so colorful, they make popular pets and are being over-collected. Plans are being made to breed them in captivity to supply the pet trade, while still preserving them in their natural habitat.

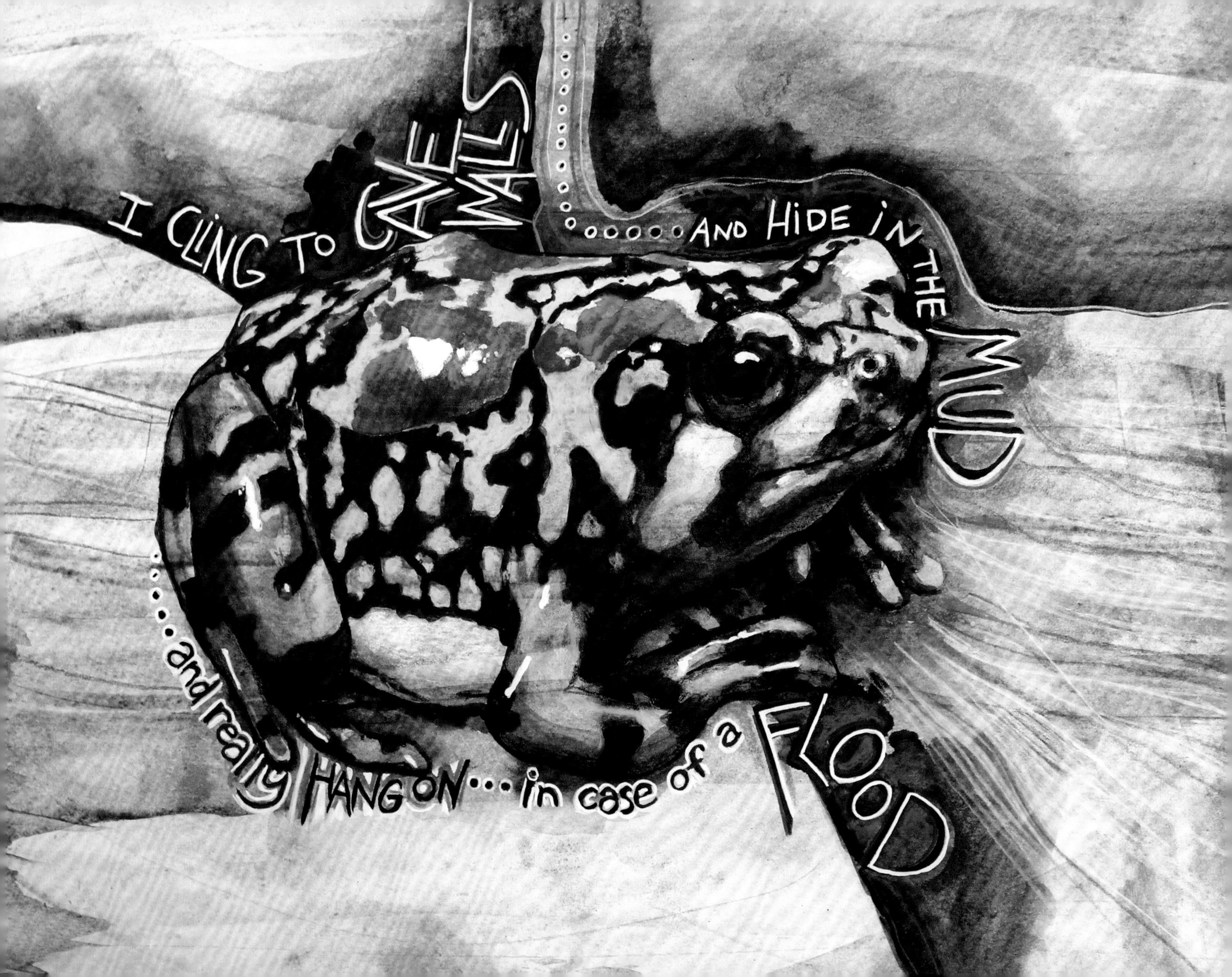
I CLING TO CAMELS
AND HIDE IN THE MUD
...and really HANG ON... in case of a FLOOD

5

Cave Salamander, or *Eurycea lucifuga*

(Reference photo by Lisa Powers)
Endangered status: LC Least Concern
Location & habitat: eastern United States

This brook salamander is well known and well-studied. It depends on limestone cave pools and aquifers, so it also depends on us to leave their waters unpolluted and their unique habitat undisturbed.

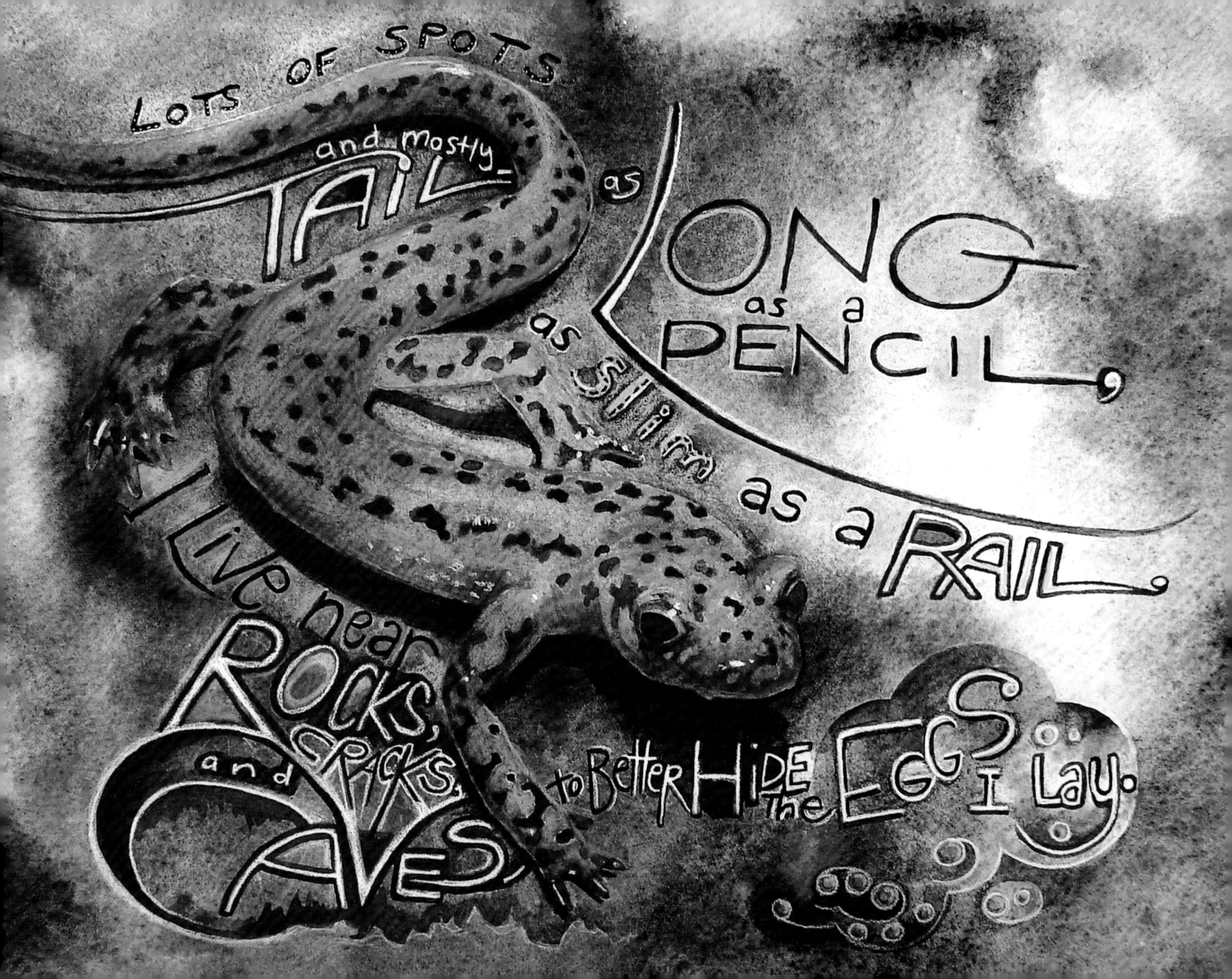
LOTS OF SPOTS
and mostly
TAIL
as LONG
as a PENCIL,
as slim as a RAIL.
I live near
ROCKS,
CRACKS,
and
CAVES
to Better HIDE the EGGS I Lay.

6

Ringed Caecilians, or *Siphonops annulatus*

Endangered status: LC Least Concern

Location & habitat: South America, as far north as Colombia and as far south as Argentina

Legless and mostly blind, the Caecilian lives underground, lays eggs, and doesn't depend on water to breed as many other amphibians do. When the babies hatch, they tear little pieces of the mother's skin off to eat. This may sound strange, but the mother isn't harmed. This is the way she feeds her kids protein-rich nutrition until they are able to find their own worms and bugs.

CAECILIANS AREN'T WORMS,
AS THEIR SKELETON CONFIRMS
LIKE SALAMANDERS with NO LEGS......
they SHED their SKIN
AND LAY EGGS.

7

Kihansi Spray Toad, or *Nectophrynoides asperginis*

(Reference photo by Rhett A. Butler)
Endangered status: EW Extinct in the wild
Location & habitat: Kihansi Falls in Tanzania

The name of the species comes from the one place where it used to live: in the spray zone on the sides of the Kihansi Falls in Tanzania. After a dam and hydroelectric plant were built upstream, the waterfall decreased to a trickle. Extra effort was taken to install sprinklers along the sides of the falls to keep them moist, but the project was unsuccessful. In just a few years, the population of toads fell from about 17,000 animals to only five. Thanks to some early collecting, today this species is still around. Breeding programs provide hope to re-introduce the species to the area.

It grows to about 5–7 millimeters long, about the size of a fingernail. The babies hatch inside their mother and are born as little gray froglets. They gradually gain more yellow color as they grow older.

A DAM UPSTREAM dried OUR WATERFALL'S SPRAY

IF IT WEREN'T FOR HUMAN HELP

WE'D ALL BE gone TODAY

8

Green Salamander, or *Aneides aeneus*

(Reference photo courtesy of the Pennsylvania Fish and Boat Commission)
Endangered status: NT Near Threatened
Location & habitat: limited areas around the Appalachian mountain range, from Ohio to Kentucky, United States.

The Green Salamander is extremely picky about where it lives. It needs completely shaded, damp rock crevices and caves in which to nest, breed, and hibernate. (Though it has occasionally been found deep under tree bark.) The mother salamander protects her eggs by guarding the entrance to the crevice ferociously. The baby salamanders emerge fully formed from their eggs. After they mature they leave home forever to – hopefully – find their own perfect new home to protect.

DOWN IN THE
DAMP
UNDER A
TREE
THERE'S
NO BETTER PLACE
FOR
ME

9

LaParva Spiny-Chested Frog, or *Alsodes Tumultuosis*

(Reference photo by Danté Fenolio)
Endangered status: CR Critically Endangered
Location & habitat: in and around the La Parva town and ski resort area, northeast of Santiago, Chile

The subfamily *Alsodinae* includes other spiny-chested frogs in Chile and Argentina. The males develop temporary spines on the chest specifically for better grip on their mate during mating season.

Have you ever seen a
FROG so SHINY?
with CHEST so SPINY?
so PLUMP?
so BRIGHT?
These SPIKES
SHOW that I'm LOOKING for my MATE...
I'M ALL dressed up
READY for a DATE.

10 | Long-Toed Salamander, or *Odorrana ishikawae* (juvenile)

(Reference photo by Martin Dollenkamp)
Endangered status: LC Least Concern*
Location & habitat: various species exist as far north as Vancouver, Canada, and as far south as Oregon, United States

These salamanders overwinter in the tadpole stage and can delay development into an adult form – sometimes waiting underwater another year until the conditions are just right.

**As a whole group, Long-toed Salamanders aren't endangered, but some isolated sub-species that are critically endangered, including the Santa Cruz Long-Toed Salamander (Ambystoma macrodactylum croceum)*

NOT QUITE READY
for LAND and AIR
I'LL LIVE
UNDERWATER
TILL the WEATHER
is
FAIR

11 | Imbabura Tree Frog, or *Hypsiboas picturatus*

(Reference photo by Brad Wilson)
Endangered status: LC Least Concern, decreasing
Location & habitat: Colombia and Ecuador

This nocturnal species is uncommon, yet there can be large populations near forested areas having streams or waterfalls. They need "closed canopy" forests to thrive – any place where the trees grow dense and provide plenty of shade. They have been found on plants and in trees with branches that hang over water.

This Rainforest Singer
smaller than your little finger
stays up late into the night
with bigger eyes for better sight.

12 Lanza's Alpine Salamander, or *Salamandra lanzai*

(Reference photo by GertJan Verspui)
Endangered status: VU Vulnerable
Location & habitat: found at higher elevations in the western Alps, near the border of France and Italy

These nocturnal, completely black salamanders live under rocks and have very long lifespans – some can live well over 20 years. They give live birth to tiny salamander babies, with no egg or tadpole stages. They also aren't dependent on permanent bodies of water, although they do like to wait until it rains to come out and play.

HIGH in the ALPS,
by STREAMS,
and UNDER STONES
YOU'LL FIND THEM...
Salamanders that LIVE for 20 YEARS
(OR LONGER, IF YOU mind THEM.)

13 The Mr. Burns Beaked Toad, or *Rhinella sp. nov.*

(Reference photo by Dr. Don Church)
Endangered status: This species is not yet classified on the IUCN Red List
Location & habitat: found in 2010, in the Chocó region of western Colombia

This is a tiny frog, at about 2 cm long. It can sit comfortably on the tip of your finger… (Oh, and it is in fact named after Monty Burns from The Simpsons television show.) Not much is known yet about this species, but the rainforests of Colombia are full of amazing and mysterious frog species like this one – some yet to be discovered.

DISCOVERED RECENTLY
THESE TOADS
WERE NAMED AFTER THEIR
POINTY NOSE

14 | Spotted Salamander, or *Ambystoma maculatum*

(Reference photo by Brian Gratwicke)
Endangered status: LC Least Concern
Location and habitat: mature forests of Canada and the Southeastern United States

Did you know that salamanders are one of the few animals that can regrow lost tissue? Scientists are studying this phenomenon, called regeneration. The process occurs through a special protein that encourages stem cell-based regrowth in the damaged area. This species relies on wild forests and ponds, and as suburbs grow it is increasingly threatened by habitat loss.

—WHEN I CAN'T GET AWAY,
AND THINGS LOOK GRIM
I CAN REGROW my TAIL
OR A NEW LIMB

15 Betic Midwife Toad, or *Alytes dickhilleni*

(Reference photo by Benny Trapp)
Endangered status: VU Vulnerable
Location & habitat: the mountains of southeastern Spain

The males are very caring fathers who take over parenting duties. He carries the fertilized eggs as they develop, until he feels them wiggle. Then he backs up and lets them hatch in a safe watery spot.

There aren't many DADDIES quite like HIM
HE CARRIES the young 'till they're READY to SWIM

16 | Giant Palm Salamander, or *Bolitoglossa dofleini*

(Reference photo by Dr. Robin Moore)
Endangered status: NT Near Threatened
Location & habitat: Guatemala and Honduras

They've adapted somewhat to humans, since they like living in cardamom plantations. However, since they take a long time to reach reproductive age (10-12 years), collecting for the pet trade may have negatively affected native populations of this salamander.

MY TONGUE
SHOOTS OUT
TO GRAB MY PREY
SO FAST
there's NO CHANCE
to GET AWAY

17 Lake Titicaca Water Frog, or *Telmatobius coleus*

(Reference photo by Brad Wilson)
Endangered status: CR Critically Endangered
Location & habitat: Lake Titicaca, on the border of Peru and Bolivia

This is a big frog – about the size of a lunch plate and weighing almost a kilogram. Its wrinkly skin helps it absorb oxygen in the water. The species is endangered because the lake has been stocked with trout (who eat the tadpoles) and the adult frogs are eaten as a local delicacy.

in the SHALLOWS of the LAKE I swim
breathing through my folds of SKIN

18 | Banded Horned Tree Frog, or *Hemiphractus fasciatus*

(Reference photo by Brian Gratwicke)
Endangered status: NT Near Threatened, decreasing
Location & habitat: along the Panamanian isthmus, in Central America

This species is very territorial, and eats other frogs - which explains its huge mouth! It's currently being bred in captivity to bring up its numbers in Panama.

HUNTING other FROGS at NIGHT—
A tiny TRAGIC TERROR
RARE, AND GETTING
HIDING UNDER LEAVES by DAY. RARER.

19 Northern Banded Newt, or *Ommatotriton ophryticus*

(Reference photo by GertJan Verspui)
Endangered status: NT Near Threatened, decreasing
Location & habitat: forest ponds and streams, along the eastern shores of the Black Sea, across Russia, Georgia, and Turkey

During courtship, the male becomes more colorfully patterned than the female. He grows a tall crest on his back and his tail becomes broader. These pretty newts are collected as pets, impacting their natural population, and are also under threat by predation from raccoons, a non-native, invasive species in this area.

this
MALE NEWT arrives WELL DRESSED
with
DOTS, SPOTS, STRIPES, and CREST.

20 Marsupial Horned Frog, or *Gastrotheca cornuta* (and two froglets)

(Reference photo by Brad Wilson)
Endangered status: EN Endangered
Location & habitat: rainforests in Colombia, Costa Rica, Ecuador and Panama

They lay the largest eggs of any amphibian, up to half an inch in diameter. The female carries these big eggs inside the brood pouch on her back. Then she gives birth to froglets, skipping the tadpole stage.

Little frog, Little frog, Little frog,
Sitting in a Tree
You never were a Tadpole.
You always looked like me.

21 California Red-Legged Frog, or *Rana draytonii*

(Reference photo by Greg Schechter)
Endangered status: VU Vulnerable
Location & habitat: coastal California and inland, into the lower Sierra Nevada mountains, United States, to as far south as Baja, Mexico

As they grow older, these frogs gradually get more and more reddish-orange (taking on a much different appearance from regular bullfrogs and toads). Tadpoles of this frog are eaten by bullfrogs, which are a non-native, invasive species in the Western United States. The California Red-Legged Frog has now been designated California's official state amphibian.

I live from SIERRAS to the SEA
despite BULLFROGS and TROUT
BUT WHAT will BECOME of MY POND
if there's drought?

22 Bornean Rainbow Toad, or *Ansonia latidisca*

(Reference photo by Ch'ien C. Lee)
Endangered status: EN Endangered
Location & habitat: around Mount Damus, Indonesia, and Mount Penrissen, Malaysia

This toad hadn't been seen at all since 1924, and none had been photographed. Remarkably three specimens of these bright, spindly toads were spotted high in a tree during a 2011 expedition called The Global Search for Lost Amphibians. It's threatened by habitat loss due to logging and the establishment of the Borneo Highlands Golf Club and Resort.

SURPRISE!
Look who's hanging around
I once was
LOST,
but now I'm
FOUND

23 Hochstetter's Frog, or *Leiopelma hochstetteri*

(Reference photo by Tony Jewell)
Endangered status: VU Vulnerable
Location & habitat: various locations across northern New Zealand

New Zealand frogs are a unique evolutionary "throwback" group. They retain many primitive features, including a lack of vocal chords, missing eardrums, and leftover tail muscles. Chytrid fungal disease is just starting to become a serious threat to these animals, as it's been discovered in neighboring frog species. Luckily, steps are being taken by the New Zealand government to protect its frogs.

YOUR ANCIENT family
has lived so LONG
without
EARS to HEAR
and NO
VOICE for a SONG

24 Rough-Skinned Newt, or *Taricha granulosa*

Endangered status: LC Least Concern

Location & habitat: Pacific coastal United States

Rough-skinned newts use a mild neurotoxin as defense against predators. One newt meal can make a hawk very sick, although raccoons and gopher snakes have developed some resistance, and still eat them. If you ever get to hold one, you should avoid touching your mouth or eyes, and wash your hands carefully afterward.

BOLDLY, I CRAWL DOWN THE TRAIL ON A MISTY MORNING.
MY ORANGE BELLY IS A WARNING—
I AM THE ROUGH-SKINNED NEWT...
SURPRISE!
WITH NEUROTOXINS THAT PARALYZE.

A note about Chytrid

While habitat destruction and loss is by far the largest threat to amphibians, if you've heard or read anything about current amphibian conservation issues you may have heard of "chytrid" or "chytridiomycosis". It's a fungal infection that is specific to amphibians, because it requires moisture to survive and spread. Often the fungus is spread to native populations by pet animals accidentally or intentionally let loose in the wild.

While we don't yet know how to protect wild amphibians or eradicate the fungus itself from nature, we can eliminate the illegal pet collection trade, which is one of the causes for current chytridiomycosis outbreaks. Also, as habitats become scarcer due to human activity, we will have to get better at caring for the amphibians that survive. International regulations already require testing to ensure that an animal is not infected before moving it across borders.

The most important thing to know about chytrid fungus is its proven destructive power. It has already caused the most severe disease-related loss of biodiversity in history. Over just the past 30 years, 200 species of frogs have been wiped out. This fungus continues to be a threat to amphibian species world-wide. Today there are more than 350 amphibian species with known chytrid infections present. It is our responsibility to know about chytrid fungus so we can better care for our amphibian friends in an uncertain future.

What can we do to help amphibians survive?

Don't buy or keep amphibians, including tadpoles, as pets. Non-native species can spread disease to wild populations, decimating them. Never set your pet "free" in the wild.

If you have a yard, don't use pesticides or herbicides. Poisons from these wash into the streams, wetlands, and lakes, causing immediate illness or indirectly disrupting the ecology of your local environment - permanently! There are plenty of alternative ways to enjoy a healthy and attractive garden.

Or, if you have a little more space, you can create a safe, educational, eco-friendly frog pond. A frog-friendly pond is about a foot deep with sloping sides, uses natural plants for filtration, and has no fish in it. Mosquitoes can be controlled naturally using time-release *Bacillus thuringiensis israelensis* floats which kill the pesky larvae. Once your pond settles, nature should take care of its own mosquito control. You don't have to put frogs in your pond! If you build it – they will come (believe it!) One more pond means one more place for native amphibian species to breed. For detailed instructions on how to make a frog pond in your yard just search online for tutorials, under the terms: "how to build a frog pond".

Learn more about endangered amphibians, and what's being done to save them, at Save the Frogs.com or Amphibian Ark.org. (And even better – spread the word about what you learn!)

THANK YOU!

In deepest gratitude - I couldn't have done it without you. Introducing the Indiegogo campaign contributors:

Adriana Weilbach
Alan Bradley
Alex Fulton
Alexa Warwick
Angela Oliver
Anita McCollum
Annalisa Moretti
April Miller
Barbara Phillips Menoche
Beth Pratt
Bill Francis
Charles Harris Doss
Charlotte Nicholson
Choti Singh
Chris Koppelberger
Christa Loren
Christine Hernandez
Conrad Seales
Cory Huff
Daniel Cole
Danielle Smeltzer
Dave Hansen
David Imhoff
David Orr
Deanna Bowser
Deb Krohn
Debra Navratil
Diane Hit
Die Booth
Ellen Lambeth
Emma Sherratt
Eric Bindseil
Erica Atreya
Erin Keuter
Fernando Pardo Urrutia
Frances Marin
Gert Jan Verspui
Grace Jackson
Hilary Lackritz
Holly Greene
Holly Koppelberger
Inara Carrillo
Ingrid Kaatz
Jaime T. Matthew
Jeff LeClere
Jen Norton
Jennifer Fritz
Jenny Loda
Jessie Rack
Jill Douglas
Jim Angley
Jim Cummings
Josie Kolf
Kalliopi Monoyios
Kerry Kriger
Kimberly Bass
Kristen Kwasek
Lacey Bryant
Laura Murphy
Leilah Thiel
Lisa Beffa
Madeleine Doiron
Margot Fass
Maria W. Bowser
Mark Jakusovszky
Martin Schulman
Matt Celeskey
Maurice Simon
Melissa Blandford
Michael C. Feher
Michael J. Harris
Michael Klieman
Michele Guieu
Matt Celeskey
Maurice Simon
Mindy Meadows
Nancy Lichtle
Neil Little
Nina Helmer
Peggy Gibbs
Rachael Hixon
Ronni Trankel
Sam Barlow
Sam Young
Samuel Shonleben
Sarah O'Brien
Shannon Amidon
Sharon Wegner-Larsen
Sienne Hayes
Stephen Johnson
Steve Racey
Steve Steuber
Teresa Jean Rich
Terry Tedesco
Sarah O'Brien
Todd Hodges
Valerie Renwick
Vic Eichler
Victor Hugo Luja Molina
Vidal
William Coleman

And dozens of additional supporters who wished to remain anonymous

SPECIAL THANKS AND ACKNOWLEDGMENTS

Dr. Kerry Kriger, Founder/Director of Save the Frogs.com

Copy Editing: Laszlo Jakusovszky and Catherine Middaugh

Reference Photography: Martin Dollenkamp, Brian Gratwicke, Ch'ien C. Lee, Rhett A. Butler, Dr. Don Church, Robin Moore, Lisa Powers, The Pennsylvania Fish and Boat Commission, Danté Fenolio, Greg Schechter, Brad Wilson, Benny Trapp, Shawn Miller, and Tony Jewell

Kalliopi Monoyios, author/editor for the Symbiartic blog at Scientific American.com

Ryan Crowder Social Media, ryancrowder.com

Made possible with a grant from CCI, **the Center for Cultural Innovation**. Their Creative Capacity Fund's "Quick Grant" program provides reimbursement funds to nonprofit organizations and individual artists in the San Francisco Bay Area and Los Angeles to enroll in workshops, attend conferences, and to work with consultants and coaches to build administrative and business skills and strengthen the economic sustainability of an organization or arts practice.